The
Animal
in the Room

Meghan
Kemp-Gee

Coach House Books, Toronto

first edition

Published with the generous assistance of the Canada Council for the Arts and the Ontario Arts Council. Coach House Books also acknowledges the support of the Government of Canada through the Canada Book Fund and the Government of Ontario through the Ontario Book Publishing Tax Credit.

LIBRARY AND ARCHIVES CANADA CATALOGUING IN PUBLICATION

Title: The animal in the room / Meghan Kemp-Gee.
Names: Kemp-Gee, Meghan, author.
Description: Poems.
Identifiers: Canadiana (print) 2022046586X | Canadiana (ebook) 20220465886 | ISBN 9781552454602 (softcover) | ISBN 9781770567542 (PDF) | ISBN 9781770567535 (EPUB)
Classification: LCC PS8621.E6265 A75 2023 | DDC C811/.6—dc23

The Animal in the Room is available as an ebook: ISBN 978 1 77056 753 5 (EPUB), ISBN 978 1 77056 754 2 (PDF)

Purchase of the print version of this book entitles you to a free digital copy. To claim your ebook of this title, please email sales@chbooks.com with proof of purchase. (Coach House Books reserves the right to terminate the free digital download offer at any time.)

To all us animals

CONTENTS

YOU SAW A DEER THROUGH BINOCULARS

after Victoria Chang's 'Barbie Chang's Daughter'

You saw a deer through binoculars. You were
a behavioural zoologist on fellowship. You were
supposed to enumerate the whole herd, but saw only
the one. The deer you caught sight of through binoculars
did not look back at you. It did not look back
at all. It moved to California. It settled
for a steady paycheque, it ran errands
in fabulously obnoxious yoga pants.
You know where this is going. But the deer
wandered into a second-hand store
off Abbot Kinney looking for
a present for a friend. It bought a pair
of second-hand binoculars. It looked
through them, second-hand.

DISAPPOINTMENT AT 9 A.M.

after Wallace Stevens's 'Disillusionment of Ten O'Clock'

The HOV lane is
moving again.
No one sees
what I see, but I see
a thing or two that's not
true about the people
in the cars merging
to inch past and
past. Not one of them
listens to old sailors
on the radio, no one sprouts antlers,
coffee-drunk, distracted, not a one
mascaras their ruminant
eyelashes. They've had enough
of low-speed crashes.
I think they all
know better.

THE FUGITIVE

We first caught sight of him lurching into
the rear-view mirror, half-obscured weaving
in between the burning blinds of sky, hills,
hot refracted sunset at our backs. Miles

and miles he tracked us, tailgating big
rigs in the passing lane, craned our necks to
check his progress, kept us thinking we'd lost
him in our blind spots or between the trees.

We accelerated into the curves
as the cruise control snaked southwest then south-
southeast across the California line.
We were watching for his headlights so we

didn't see what lurched into our way, lit
up in the fast lane not knowing which way to run.

DISAPPOINTMENT AT 10 A.M.

In Santa Monica, the yoga teachers say things like *Practise gratitude* and *We are spiritual beings having a physical experience.* They say *Deep belly breathing* and *Form before depth.* Meanwhile, something with cloven feet and big bad teeth crawls in quadruped from Main Street. It's here to practise its deep breathing with wet nose pressed against the steamed-up windows. It has come to watch the class and ask us some questions about exactly what kind of experience it is supposed to have.

THE LETTER OF RECOMMENDATION

I coached the applicant for four years on the UCLA club team. She demonstrated outstanding leadership qualities. She volunteered, she shone. She asked smart questions. Whenever something went wrong, she'd want to know what to do differently. She'd want to know exactly what she could have done.

NEWFANGLENESS

I have seen them gentle, tame, and meek,
That now are wild and do not remember
                              – Thomas Wyatt

You are remembering her wrong.
Between the time when she ate bread from
your hand and where you find her now
there is so much distance, so much
space. There is the room where everything
happened. There is how you recall
it, there are bread crumbs in your hand,

and there is everything between.
Twenty times is better, but once
especially, the space between
having and not having, the ounce
of difference. Yes, just the once
is best. You're remembering wrong.
She is long and small. She is wrung

out. She's leaving something out,
some detail. It's not kindness,
this detail she's leaving out.
She forgot to mention it. Best
that you let it go mentionless
yourself. She is small and long. She is
not wrong. You're not deserving, but she is.

SADDLESTITCHING I

If your   fingers hurt

      if there's

wax under   the nails

      if you

feel callus   if your

      hands pulled

the thread   tight one

      or two

hundred thousand   times then

      maybe learn

a thing   or two

      from where

you binded   bound or

      bind together

crossed over   one thing

                    then two

or maybe   learn to

            wind up

wind down   your life

            like cars

coming down   Coldwater Canyon

            cut real

close to   the leather

            get paid

cash under   the table

            then burn

the endings   one and

            two.

THE BRONTOSAURUS

I want the future to remake my life.
I want them to find my scattered pieces
in Wyoming. I want them to fix a
camarasaurus skull to the end of

my tail and I want Othniel Charles
Marsh to give me a fabulous new name.
I want them to fill my mouth with pig teeth
and call me Nebraska Man, I want them

to debate the significance of my
feathers in their journals, I want Steven
Spielberg to direct the movie, I want
Charles Darwin to feast on my flesh at

Cambridge University, and I want
fundamentalists to call me a hoax.

THE GIANT PACIFIC OCTOPUS

If you're hungry for wisdom, write your proverbs in dead languages;
they're dangerous in living mouths. If threatened, flee. If you can't run,
hide your softness tight against sharp rock; when you can't hide,
    blend in, make
your hide lovely rippled sand and diamond-grained granite. If you can't
blend in, draw blood. Write your riddles at right angles or with sensuous
bonelessness; there is no happy medium. Wise men seeking advice
from happy mediums should not expect to be happy themselves.
The mindless mind their own business best. I mind mine by watching you.

THE VANCOUVER ISLAND MARMOT

we will send
out a look
out we will
send one of
us one of
all twenty
one of us
one or two
of us know
a thing or
two about
how it is
an island
can be a
lifeboat a
life can be
a lifeboat
too and one
of us can
keep all of
us afloat
all afloat
we will send
one of us
out to have
a look

THE GREENLAND SHARK

Slow, slow
as anything, my life,
my autopsy, my

stomach
slit and spitting up sweet
mandibles of my

last love,
my juvenile polar
bear, my unknown one,

his un-
known fate only I know,
the day I found I

knew him
in deep water, deep as
night, how late one night

he, his
salt-logged hairs suspended
like his four long limbs,

dearest
emaciated, hung
in his tremendous

slowness,
elegant descent, to
me so slow, my love

and his
million-dollar ribs drawn
gorgeous, glowing with

a crown
of illuminated
arthropods, his holy

slowness,
his hundred-hour cascade
from ice to love four-

hundred-
year me, I loved him, found
him, only I know.

AFTER THE ARCHER

The other day I thought to ask after
you. You were always my favourite, so I
meant to ask where I could find you, or how
much time had passed since we misremembered
each other's numbers. But I always liked
this force propelled from good catgut to fletch
to poaching deer on the king's lands, and that's
the question I asked. But really I was
thinking how I'd misremembered you, how
my heart's plastic got nocked and windowed, how
you always really were my favourite, how
you always looked great in profile and cut
the rope when no one was looking and rode
the chandelier as it came crashing down.

BISHOP

I respect your religious convictions
and I believe you when you say you were
on a Greyhound bus over red-gravel
Nova Scotia roads and saw a curious
moose cow tower in your childish headlights.
I believe that you were who you say you
are, that when you use the word *I* you are
using it to mean what it needs to mean.
I believe equally easily in
your memory of the sound of rain and what
you mean when you say *wake up together,*
wake each other up to belief without
thinking and find it is a marvel to
mean that I believe in everything you say.

THE IRRADIATED ORB-WEAVER SPIDERS

They wrote a scientific
article about our new faith

in shapes and tastes that came in
on the rain and they said we were

apostates when they did not see
the perfect desiccated husks

of aphids giving themselves
up and silver pooling in foot-

prints in mud on blue mornings
becoming hunger when we and

we alone received the blue-
prints for our reconstruction and

dreamed it wet and dense against
our wingtips, breathing heavy in our hands.

YOU EMAILED ME YOUR RESUMÉ

You were looking for different
words to say *good team player*. I
suggested you use more verbs. I
suggested you say you *over-*

saw the team. I suggested you
call me. Together, we practised
for the part of the interview
where they ask if you have any

questions. I have a question. My
question is what team do we play
for. My question is what did you
do, did you *manage* or *over-*

see, my question is what did you
oversee, my question is why do we keep
using the same words and how would
a wolf talk and what would it say.

WHERE IT HAPPENED

The room that you paid for
where everything happened
while the dark came down out-
side and the number twelve
bus went by knows a thing
or two about having
someone's number, knows how
to watch its weight, knows its
eighth-grade science, makes some
calculations about
mass and gravity, but
see how the dust hovers
all the same two inches
above the wooden floor.

COACHING

The secret to good defence, I tell her, is once someone does something to you once, you never let them do it again.

THE WOLF EMAILED ME ITS RESUMÉ

works well with others   magna
no, summa   no, magna cum laude
feels at home   in competitive,
fast-paced work environments   no,

thrives in   highly structured, close-knit
work environments   should i say
team, community   or should i
say environment   should i say

highly specialized   harder than
bone   the one who went in first when
it heard the herd-lost   calf call out,
certificate program   master

of business   administration
highly motivated   who went
in second when   it smelled the coat
dyed red   words per minute

experience with excel   and
java   executed special
projects   stumbled home the morning
after wearing someone   else's

clothes   went in first and never
once fell behind   not ever

BIKING TO WORK

Stalking car doors and potholes, I like to say it's not my fault if the road grows rashes or if calves go missing. I am a creature that will drown the whole city in sheepskin and lie on both sides of the bed. I wear a helmet, I take the lane. The West Side taught me how to pedal hard and lie this way. *Safety third*, I like to joke. I wear a helmet, herd mentality, big bad teeth. The roadkill looks both ways, claws and antlers west to Venice Beach, felling careless deer across the sharrows, lanes, and shoulders. I wear a helmet and I tell lies. I'm pretending that I don't know better.

OPOSSUM HOUR

The helicopters flush
them out from underbrush
detritus and underpass cracks to trot
imperiously along

the subdivision walls.
If you were walking home
alone, this is the time of night when you
might take a shortcut through

a back alley somewhere
in Mid-City. You might
hear what sounds like sirens or stray fireworks,
footsteps or the neighbour's

baby still awake and
singing its ABCs.
You might look up and see a pair of eyes
hovering at chest height

flushed and filled with light in
defiance or raised
in ignorance. You might see them bristle
and twitch in the beating

air from overhead. You
might hurry past, you might
take another path, but either way, you're
getting away alone.

IN THE FACE

It has grey eyes. It has
brown and green
eyes. See, it lives just out
of frame. See,
it's better and it's worse
to learn to
recognize the ways that
faces change
when you're not looking. It's
not the thing
that you set out to say.

You set out to say it,
say the thing
that you weren't looking at.
Faces change
in ways you recognize.
Come learn how
it's better and it's worse
in frame, see
wild eyes, see brown
and green eyes,
grey eyes, the same two things.

P-41

Your four children, two captured and
two road-murdered,
half-survive you, everywhere fenced
in but never
spotted, only once collared but
often captured
in their motion-activated film
traps, survivor
of brush fire and rat poison, quick
coyote killer,
Sunset Canyon prowler, canny
photogenic
brook-finder, last half-father, old
recluse of the
Verdugos, good watchman of the
210 freeway.

THE HALFTIME HUDDLE

Pay better attention, I tell them, to which way you turn your hips and head. Keep your back to the sideline. You want to be able to see what's coming. You want to be able to keep an eye on everything.

WHOSO LIST I

Two hundred million handguns, one or two
hundred stranded tide pools full of orange
cucumbers, twenty thirty-five-year-old
revolutionaries, the twenty bowls
of split pea soup they eat for dinner, one
or two stories about a wise old king
with many clever daughters, eleven
of which daughters wake up wanting
to tell someone about the strange thing they've
just dreamed, two deer in the headlights, once or
twice a week I dream about getting shot
in the mouth a dozen times and sitting
still, feeling the bullets trapped forever
bouncing around forever trapped inside.

WHOSO LIST II

I am the High Sheriff of Kent. My desires
and who desires them draw, feint, and flee
extraordinarily. Sometimes they'll name
rebellions after me. Sometimes I write
and what I write has deer in it. I am
deer-bitten, hind-infested, bound up in
ungulation. I watch the same movies
again and again because I forget
the endings. I like sword-and-sandal ones
where you see the soldiers' thighs and women
stolen by stop-motion monsters. I am
the Ambassador. I build embassies
then burn them down again but not before
I lock the civil servant deer inside.

WHOSO LIST III

I am the High Sheriff of Kent. I am your father.
I am a red sunburned colonial explorer
in a brand-new land. I give the land a name, invent
it out of its inhabitants. I am a tall young

poet locked in a room with a particular view
of the tower courtyard. I am the anointed head
of state, I am the supreme governor of the church,
I eat most prodigiously. I eat roast venison

in mid-winter. I eat six-fingered animals and
never gain an ounce. Once or twice it happens I have
been complimented on my broad-stanced accomplishments.
I am the perfect candidate. I have brought with me

an extra copy of my resumé. I have since
banished the previous inhabitants to France. I have
wrestled my curriculum vitae out of their six-
fingered hands. I hear there is a new lizard species

just now being discovered. They will name it after
me. I am going hunting, I am playing my old
hunting games again. I will look it in the eyes. There,
I will rediscover exactly what I am.

STRENGTH AND CONDITIONING

Lift heavy, I keep telling them. Form before depth, knees over toes, lower abdominals engaged. *Crouching tiger*, I find myself saying. *Strong is fast.* If we don't want to get hurt, I find myself saying, we need big strong legs, to keep us safe. *You want to be able to,* I find myself saying, *deadlift your own weight.* So make sure you're *getting enough protein.* This whole time, the team captain's been taking notes. She raises her hand. She has a question. She says, *So you mean we should eat more meat.*

THE TRAPLINES

Once there was a snowstorm,
heart-stoppingly cold and

Once you felt it, you were
doomed not to be the same.

Once you stumbled in, you
began to change your face.

Once we wrapped you up in
sheepskins to thaw, I thought

Once, or maybe I thought
twice. Once or twice I thought

Once you were inside I
should ask where you came from.

Once I'd thought about it
I saw it was too late.

THE OLD WOMAN WHO ATE AND ATE

I peddled miles of traplines east of Portage la Prairie.
One time there was a storm. I toddled and I tripped half-dead
for days until I found where an old woman lived alone
with her lovely red-haired daughter in a clearing of the trees.
I offered terms. I peddled shelter, changed my faces, slept
straight for two nights and one day. The old wife saw me boil and
dream-burn. While I huddled by the stove I think I saw her
watch me with her teeth. When I woke the second night I think
I found myself choking on bile and digging in a dawn-
lit snowbank, found myself limping cold-sick unsatisfied
back toward the fire. She never spoke of her lost daughter,
but the third night she gave me slick and briny things to drink.
I peddled miles of traplines east of Portage la Prairie.
I lifted up the witch's skirts and saw her cloven feet.

HER DAUGHTER

Once my mother told me an old story. You can take the worst
thing you ever did. You can name a deer after it. The deer's
name won't be yours anymore. Through the trees you can watch it from
a distance. You can let it get away from you. Here's the piece

of my red hair you wanted to bring home with you. Here's the worst
thing you ever did. In your youth they taught you that the duty
of a host is holy. I invented curses like lost toes
in storms for bad mid-winter guests. May your body's fibres

spread like antlers may your knuckles split like roots of trees may your
hot voraciousness outlive your bones and traplines. Our ending
and your eating do not belong to any kind of story.

There's not a name for my place in the clearing. There's no story
for your stormed-in fevered viciousness. There's no name for the old
thing that raised me. There's no mythology. You don't deserve that.

THE ANIMALS IN THE ROOM

You drank too much. The animals came into the room.
They saw your path to the exit blocked. Their herd sense
calculated one or two escape routes, attuned
tick-bitten ears on your behalf to the exact
moment when you could have spoken up, turned an art
appraiser's eye to silence, threw themselves into
the painting on the wall, the deer with hard black eyes
and one bright painful spot of blue in them. They came
into the room. Your terror wanted them to watch
what happened and your terror saw the blue spot and
your terror got a lichen-eating audience
to your bull's-eye focus on that blue-stained motel
deer's-eye, your terror drank too much, your eyes summoned
them, they saw your story shrink into a fist.

IXODES SCAPULARIS

The almighty made
us a flea-bitten
world. The cretaceous
witch's slick lyme curse
invented other
kinds of bites, vector
and kingdom and nymph.

The almighty made
a perfect world for
hair-legged subclasses
to wrap their eightfold
selves around. We take
hosts, take our blood meal
in each stage of life.

TEACHING COMPOSITION

I compare a satisfying sentence to the feeling of kicking somebody as hard as you can, square in the chest. The kid in the back row asks, *Have you actually done that?*

THE HOTEL ROOM

In the hotel you get drunk and watch movies on HBO, a period piece and back-to-back buddy cops. This hotel room is not a room where anything bad has ever happened to you. For the rest of your life, every room will be a room where nothing has happened yet. Things happen once and don't happen again. Every room you will ever be in will be a new, brave-peopled world. The remote control on the corner of the bed will do the right thing in the third act. The ice bucket is a bit of a loose cannon. Your wake-up call calls in a 10-91. The buzzing lamp will beg its sensible live-in girlfriend to take it back, the stain on the ceiling complains that it doesn't get paid enough for this shit. The hand towels have the wrong taste in music but everybody learns to get along in the end. The empty bottles complain about the bad coffee at the precinct. The front desk calls and apologizes once and for all for any inconvenience. The room opens up and offers you everything. They should call an exterminator. There are animals moving behind the walls.

DR. OPPENHEIMER, DVM

after Anna Leahy's 'The Day of Fire and Light'

The spectacled veterinarian
diagnosed the deer with a heart defect,
a leaky valve that quivered and murmured
louder than she would have liked. She seemed kind

and stroked the jewel-like flea bites in its tick-
pricked coat. With the right treatment it might live.
She seemed very qualified. We saw her
framed diploma on the wall. We heard how

the quirks of its genome rolled off her tongue.
She left us with the distinct impression
nothing else needed to be said. There is
a popular misconception that hearts

beat like poetry. She tattooed this on
its skin. She stitched up its arrow-riddled
hide. She prescribed it baby aspirin as
she shone a penlight in its wolf-shy eyes.

Through her syntax and diction, the author explores her main theme in a clear and effective way. Through the use of rhetorical devices including metaphor and repetition, the writer emphasizes her argument. Throughout this poem, the meaning is reflected by the form in several ways. In this text, the author has some questions and she asks them using various rhetorical techniques and narrative strategies. In the poem, the use of various strategies enhances the meaning overall. Overall, in this poem, the meaning is enhanced and emphasized through the poet's use of form. Through the use of language, repetition, and syntax, the poet has some questions for you about what exactly happened here and who is supposed to pay for what.

A NEWLY DISCOVERED SPECIES OF LIZARD WITH DISTINCTIVE TRIANGULAR SCALES

I am Charles Darwin. I eat owl flesh at Cambridge University.
I have discovered something, an entirely new species
with tropical fever in its reptile fingers. I am busy
with taxonomizing its most peculiar and three-sided
armour, its six-toed fitness for these latitudes and its perfect
speckled eggs like forlorn love notes, black mammalian eyes pinpricked
with blue as if caught in headlights, suddenly. I've isolated
a cold-weathered ancestor in its DNA. I'm going to clone
its terrible antlered children, its swarming descendants, outsource
its coiled vertebrate progenitors to secret facilities
hungry for fresh IP. I've obtained Steven Spielberg to direct
the lizard's biography. I will name it after royalty. I am
deliriously pleased. I find myself full of discovery.
I am homesick, boat-sick. I am hotel-room-sick. I want to go home.

THE PALEONTOLOGIST

Othniel Charles Marsh, b. 1831, put on
a pinafore and spent the day plucking out new themes
at the pianoforte. He had one last question
concerning wolves. If a wolf had something to say, what
would it be? Othniel Charles Marsh was a notorious
anatomist and shameless discoverer of new
species. He once spliced his whole life onto a love poem
from the sixteenth century. He wrote science fiction
under a pen name and he reinvented every
hotel room he stayed in for the rest of his life. Once,
in 1864, he ate two slices of cake
on someone else's birthday. He indulged outrageous
rivalries. He stole his opponents' bones. He dug up
fragments in the desert and put all the skulls on wrong.

INTRODUCTION TO CREATIVE NON-FICTION

I don't know what to write about, the kid in the back row says. *Can I write an essay about how my mom grows orchids?* I tell him you're allowed to write about anything, as long as you're pretty sure it's true. *Did you know that orchids are a parasite?* he asks. I say I think I did know that.

THE BLOODSUCKER

I have a question
for the ticks who dream
about being wolves.
My question concerns
orchids and the end
of the world, concerns
the colour blue and
rare diseases. I

am going to ask
about your dreams, am
asking after your
desires, your mothers,
past lives, heavenly
tastes and white-tailed hosts.

THE GOLIATH BIRDEATER

I ate an owl once. My life is stuffed full
of dreams. My life has an eye for wonder.
I've seen the Almighty in the wet orb
of a terrified lizard's black right eye.
I think I'm going to stow away across
the Atlantic Ocean in organic
banana crates to study some applied
human anatomy at Cambridge
University. I think I'll become
a poet. I'll write love poems about
songbirds. I'll get a job uncrating
the bananas in a distribution
warehouse. I'll write the love poems on my lunch
breaks and work too hard for minimum wage.

LUCY

A slice is missing from her right shin bone. Her other
name means 'You Are Marvellous' in Amharic. They all
wax poetic about the angle of her knee joints,
the spread of her pubic arch, her muscular jaws and
wide rib cage, her Pliocene diet, her beautiful
red hair. She was buried in a snowbank due north of
the Assiniboine in 1843. Twelve years
ago, biology students on a field trip
found traces of a wandering peddler's traps. No one found
his femurs. No one studied the slant of his pelvis
at Case Western University. Before the oaks
and aspen parklands mossed and rotted him to nothing,
scavengers notched their canines on the plains and corners
of his exposed scapulas, his load-bearing plateaus.

THE WOLF MAKES AN APPOINTMENT AT THE OB/GYN

I just had some quick questions. I was just calling for a routine checkup. My first question is what are you saying. My next question is what do you mean by contraindication. What do you mean by sexual preference. What exactly are you offering me and can I avoid eye contact and can I say no thank you and

Look, is this one of those things where the story's author finds itself complicit because I was just asking questions I was not following orders I was just writing things down and I didn't ask for any of this. It's not my fault if the cattle don't keep track of their numbers, it's not up to me whose clothes I'm wearing and if fawns go missing. What I am asking is,

Look, it was just body language. It doesn't mean anything. I'm just saying I was hungry, it was just a hotel room I paid for. I was only baring my teeth for show.

COPY-EDITING

'Begging the question' is a logical fallacy. I think you mean 'raising the question.' As usual, this raises some questions. As usual, this begs for questions of my own. My questions beg for more questions. They whine, they whistle. They want your attention. They are biting at your heels and bristling. They want to be let out, to be begged for, to be let in.

THE BEAST OF GÉVAUDAN

I like peasant women
in dirty petticoats. In winter when the ground
is frozen and the sky is clear, exquisite how I leave no footprints, how

I take down fertile deer.
I pluck rabbits sweetly hibernating from ice-
insulated burrows. I like executions carried out at dawn and

watching from a distance,
the feeling of fine-laced pale aristocracy.
I like influence at my fingertips, I like pornography. I like

sending purloined letters,
I like sealing the folds in the paper with hot
red wax. I like keeping myself just out of sight, licking the cold packed earth

from my skin's deep creases,
the smell of rabbits, hard exquisite winter sky.

CROCODILE WITH BUTTERFLY

For our blooming crowns
of sipping guests, our
grinning hot-skinned hosts,
parched stillness between
startling, swimming, sun-
basks between sex and
famine, your breathless
quick-lipped shivering
like questions, like your
laughter, your violets,
your temples bound with
purple flowers, wet
rumours, their sweetness,
your tears, their salt.

DEER WITH RAVEN

Am I weak, she asks her. Will the world weaken me
or will I be nourished
by pieces of the world. Her wet eyes reflecting
white as she alights from
a dense low winter sky, she cuts out a black splash.
Her skull sprouts knuckles, springs
downy branches, hitches slick wings like spread fingers.

When she retires at night
she frames the X-rays in her roost. She contemplates
backlit homologous
anatomy in our forelimbs, gleans this meaning:
If you fall down in mid-
winter, I will be first to visit where your small
carcass landed in the snow.

SADDLESTITCHING II

With the thread sweetly waxed and sweeter, your leather and daily bread, your two needles, shell cordovan, the needles, the blisters, the fire at the end, rich pull-up in full aniline, the dives and crosses, cavalier and dublin, hard give and slip of harness and bridle measured twice, cut quickly and left to darken in the sun, the give and slip and rows of empty holes like spaces between fir trees across one or two hundred thousand miles, the pine beetles drying out the century inside them, the crow crossing them in winter catching sight of fallen deer.

OFFICE HOURS

They say, I want to know how to do better. I am applying to medical school next year, so I need to make sure I have perfect grades. I was wondering, they say, if we could go over the next essay assignment. I know this paragraph doesn't make sense. I don't know what point I'm trying to make. I ask them, What are you really trying to say? They say, I am still adjusting to my medication. They say, Last week I went to the emergency room. Do you know what a panic attack is? I tell them that I think I do. They say, I feel like I have to choose between feeling stupid and feeling scared all the time. I say, I feel like we can figure out this paragraph. I'll ask you some more questions and then we'll figure out what you were trying to say.

THE WOLF RETURNS YOUR CALL

It has a question.
It wants to know what
you mean when you say
seem. For example,
when they say that *You*
don't seem *like yourself,*
it does not know what
seeming is, so it
can't tell. You tell it
this is a question
of taxonomy.
This is a question,
this is not a pet.
This is a question,
a wild animal.
Do not touch the bars.
Keep your hands to your-
self. Come home wearing
someone else's clothes.
Don't be mistaken.
What do they mean by
Do not feed. Do you
understand what that
means. Do you find it
confusing for some
reason, when it licks
your face and asks you
questions. What happened,
it asks. You're crying.
What does crying mean.

AVOIDING THE PASSIVE VOICE

It is shown and it is being argued. It is easily understood and related to. It can be argued, it can be seen. What's happening here? I ask. What exactly can be seen?

I'm trying to explain that the real problem isn't passive voice, per se, but the absence of a grammatical subject. Why don't you want to say who's arguing or understanding? Why are you so afraid to say when you're the one who sees?

The kid in the front row says, Our high school English teacher said we weren't allowed to use the word *I*.

That's a good point, I say. Sometimes that's not allowed. So that's a whole other problem. That is a problem that is easily seen and related to by me.

AFTER THE STORM

The freeway underpasses
will be a good place
to decide the new
anatomy, what each part

means. The heart was once the seat
of love. Now it will
be the liver, or
love will live in the fingers.

The liver will be the seat
of envy. Envy's
fingers will filter
through the bile. And our sorrow

will live in our stomachs, growl
after the storm. Late
invasive species
will get seats at the table.

The fauna gets a little
wild. Wolves will live like
lost dogs. They will live
in Los Angeles and hold

their meetings under on-ramps.
They'll bury the old
stories our bodies
are now holding in reserve.

LA ZONE ROUGE

The green circles around the craters come up hearty,
        crisp with borrowed calcium. The rapeseed thanks
the bones of wounded horses put point-blank to sleep in
        1917. For the deer thriving with
hundred-year-old heavy metals in their livers, boars
        bright-eyed and manning ivied trenches, and for
arsenic-drunk wildcats tripping their vole hunts around
        undetonated canisters: We have been
dropping in on you. Yesterday the deminers dug
        out a Saint-Chamond, lovely and rusted down
to red-brown lace. To the amphibians, to all those
        chlorinated orchids whom it may concern:
We are planning a solar farm in Bezonvaux. We
        left behind a signpost where there used to be
a fountain. Here stood the church, a school there. We'll see
        you soon, voici pour votre santé. Attention:
Keep well out of sight another seven centuries.

HOMILY FOR THE RADIOACTIVE BOARS OF PRIPYAT

God lives in bodies
too toxic for consumption in
carcasses unsafe

for human touch God resides
on a cellular
level where things reside in that

dual sense we think
that God lives once and once or twice
happens once then once

again and this particular
beauty lives in our
hunger among scotch pines between

feasts of acetate-
pumped mushrooms buzzing and twisting
like the red forest's

orb weavers' webbed apostasy
like the hero dead
for no good reason and dying

again the beauty
of readers across vast distance
all weeping at once

weeping at the same time and this
half-life is the twice-
living of God of blackcaps and

acacias and of
abandoned barns and foraged
sacks of salvaged grain

rooting them open ripping through
and feasting and of
our loneliness our time alone

with God our sweetly
sated hunger and our twenty
thousand years to go.

THE AMERICAN HORSESHOE CRAB

Imagine the whole world
wanting you. Imagine
farm labs and factories,
test tubes flash-boiled clean.

Imagine infection
drowning in pale blue milk,
imagine all of us
hovering and clotting

in your blood. Imagine
us suspended in gel
and sold distilled, prescribed
contaminated with

your Jurassic proteins,
the wrack line at high tide.

THE NORTH ATLANTIC RIGHT WHALE

If you're interested in terms like *colony collapse,*
negative feedback cycle, die-off, vessel
strike, apocalypse, or *functionally extinct,*
you're in the right place. I'm an authority.

My expertise is in saying goodbye, just
in case. Facing the knowledge that you might not
meet again, better to take matters into
your own hands. Better your own hands rather than

find yourself alone, find you've spoken your last
words without knowing it. Better not listen
for echoes, better not hear the hard answers
about your own longevity. Better swim

too shallow. Better test the bedrock, drum your
knuckles on the shorebreak. Better not to know.

THE LIAR

Saying that something has happened once is not a prediction that it will happen twice. This is something I have often said. I am trying to keep saying it. I am pretending that I don't know better.

THE TRAIN HOME

On the train there are people with all kinds of minds. They're going home to all kinds of rooms designed by different kinds of architects. There are architects who call the future a storm and then there are architects who as children read a book about a wise old king who had eleven clever daughters. One daughter died at a tragically young age but was remembered bittersweetly. They still name things after her, like dawns and trains. One daughter promised never to marry until a man bested her in single combat. One daughter kept exotic chickens and named them after famous actors. One daughter stayed out too late in the wrong kind of moonlight and was transformed into a white-tailed deer. One wore yellow shoes every day of her life. One spoke only in cracks and rustles because she wanted to preserve the native language of endangered trees. One was a calligrapher and spent decades contemplating the delicious commonalities between the words *clever* and *eleven*. One was a great mathematician-philosopher who wrote a celebrated treatise on the question of whether things happen twice or whether they only really happen once. One was an explorer and a naturalist who wrote about her adventures, then buried the books in the ground so only advanced civilizations could read them, in the future after the storm. One daughter should have been twin daughters but she ate her sister in the womb. The last and youngest daughter was a poet, and in his wisdom the old king counted his blessings and banished her forever.

NOTES

p. 9: Victoria Chang's 'Barbie Chang's Daughter' appears in her 2017 collection *Barbie Chang*.

p. 10: Wallace Stevens's 'Disillusionment of Ten O'Clock' appeared in his 1923 collection *Harmonium*.

pp. 14, 34–36: Thomas Wyatt's 'They Flee from Me' and 'Whoso List to Hunt' were first printed in 1557. It is possible that, while imprisoned in the Tower of London on charges of adultery, Wyatt witnessed the 1536 execution of Anne Boleyn.

p. 17: Othniel Charles Marsh was a founding figure in the field of pale-ontology, famous for his discovery of a vast number of extinct species and his fierce rivalry with Edward Drinker Cope. In 1883, he 'invented' the brontosaurus by putting a camarasaurus head on an apatosaurus body. In 1917, paleontologist Henry Fairfield Osborn 'invented' Nebraska Man, a now-debunked North American hominid, after he misidentified some fossilized pig teeth.

p. 19: The Vancouver Island marmot is a great conservation success story; after its numbers dropped below thirty animals in 2003, there may be as many as three hundred alive today.

p. 20: The Greenland shark is the world's longest-living vertebrate. Some individuals may live as long as five centuries. Autopsies of sharks have revealed that their diet sometimes includes small polar bears.

p. 22: Errol Flynn starred in *The Adventures of Robin Hood* in 1938.

p. 23: 'Bishop' references Elizabeth Bishop's 'The Moose' and 'It Is Marvellous to Wake Up Together.'

p. 24: The irradiated orb-weaver spiders in the Red Forest near Chernobyl have been observed weaving their webs in strange patterns, even decades after the disaster.

p. 29: 'Biking to Work' contains two lines from Thomas Middleton and Thomas Dekker's play *The Roaring Girl*, first published in 1611.

p. 30: 'Opossum Hour' references Elizabeth Bishop's 'The Armadillo' and Robert Lowell's 'Skunk Hour.'

p. 32: The body of famous Los Angeles mountain lion P-41 was discovered in the Verdugo Mountains in 2017 with rat poison in his stomach.

p. 45: Anna Leahy's 'The Day of Fire and Light' was first published in *Drunken Boat* in 2013.

p. 47: While at Cambridge University, Charles Darwin served as president of the Glutton Club, organizing the cooking and eating of unusual fowl, including hawks, bitterns, and a tawny owl.

p. 51: The Goliath birdeater is the largest spider in the world. It eats various small amphibians, mammals, reptiles, insects, and (occasionally) birds.

p. 52: The remains of AL 288-1, or 'Lucy,' were discovered in 1974 in Ethiopia and returned there in 2013.

p. 55: In the 1760s, an unidentified animal or group of animals killed hundreds of people in the French province of Gévaudan.

p. 63: The Zone Rouge is a group of highly contaminated areas defined by the French government as impossible for human life after World War I. Unexploded ordnance, human remains, and heavy metal contamination will make the Zone Rouge inhospitable for tens of thousands of years.

p. 66: The bright blue blood of the American horseshoe crab is an essential ingredient in the manufacturing and testing of vaccines. It is one of the world's most valuable natural resources.

p. 67: The North Atlantic right whale is one of the world's most endangered species, with a population of under twenty individuals remaining, and shrinking fast.

ACKNOWLEDGEMENTS AND THANKS

Thank you to the editors who published versions of these poems.

'The Greenland Shark' was in *EcoTheo Review*. 'You Emailed Me Your Resumé,' 'The Wolf Emailed Me Its Resumé,' 'The Animals in the Room,' 'The Wolf Makes an Appointment at the OB/GYN,' and 'The Wolf Returns Your Call' were in *Anomaly*. 'The Wolf Makes an Appointment at the OB/GYN,' 'The Hotel Room,' 'The Wolf Returns Your Call,' 'After the Storm,' and 'The Train Home' were in *Eunoia Review*. 'Disappointment at 9 a.m.,' 'Opossum Hour,' and 'P-41' were published in the *Altadena Poetry Review*. 'A Newly Discovered Species of Lizard with Distinctive Triangular Scales' was in *Plenitude Magazine*. 'Copy-Editing' was in the *lickety~split*.

In 2022, 'The Fugitive' appeared in *Shooter Literary Magazine*; 'The Giant Pacific Octopus' and 'The Vancouver Island Marmot' were in *Channel Mag*.

Thank you to my teacher Anna Leahy, who generously read the earliest versions of this book.

Thank you to my editor, Susan Holbrook, for her care and encouragement – and for encouraging me to add a few more poems.

Thank you to my family, for all of your love and support, and to my teachers and students, for supporting and inspiring me.

And to James, my favourite archer: thank you, love.

Meghan Kemp-Gee writes poetry, comics, and scripts of all kinds. She has also worked as a writing teacher, screenplay consultant, and ultimate Frisbee coach. She received her BA from Amherst College and MA and MFA from Chapman University. She currently lives somewhere between Vancouver and Fredericton, where she is a PhD student at the University of New Brunswick.

Typeset in Arno and Wayfinder.

Printed at the Coach House on bpNichol Lane in Toronto, Ontario, on Zephyr Antique Laid paper, which was manufactured, acid-free, in Saint-Jérôme, Quebec, from second-growth forests. This book was printed with vegetable-based ink on a 1973 Heidelberg KORD offset litho press. Its pages were folded on a Baumfolder, gathered by hand, bound on a Sulby Auto-Minabinda, and trimmed on a Polar single-knife cutter.

Coach House is on the traditional territory of many nations, including the Mississaugas of the Credit, the Anishnabeg, the Chippewa, the Haudenosaunee, and the Wendat peoples, and is now home to many diverse First Nations, Inuit, and Métis peoples. We acknowledge that Toronto is covered by Treaty 13 with the Mississaugas of the Credit. We are grateful to live and work on this land.

Edited by Susan Holbrook
Cover design by Crystal Sikma
Interior design by Crystal Sikma
Author photo by Wade Andrew

Coach House Books
80 bpNichol Lane
Toronto ON M5S 3J4
Canada

416 979 2217
800 367 6360

mail@chbooks.com
www.chbooks.com